POCKET IMAGES

Barry

POCKET IMAGES

Barry

Geoffrey A. North

NONSUCH

To Elaine, for her patience and encouragement.

Also, to my grandchildren
with the sincere wish
that they too will find pleasure in their heritage.

Front cover: Passengers on the PS *Barry*, 29 August 1908

First published 1996
This new pocket edition 2005
Images unchanged from first edition

Nonsuch Publishing Limited
The Mill, Brimscombe Port,
Stroud, Gloucestershire, GL5 2QG
www.nonsuch-publishing.com

British Library Cataloguing in Publication Data.
A catalogue record for this book is available from the British Library.

ISBN 1-84588-129-X

Typesetting and origination by Nonsuch Publishing Limited
Printed in Great Britain by Oaklands Book Services Limited

Contents

Introduction

Barry has always held a certain fascination for me and I was thrilled to be asked to contribute a book on Barry to the Archive Photographs series.

My mother, Jean North (née James), was born in Barry and, as a child, I spent many happy hours visiting relatives in the town, as well as enjoying frequent trips to the beach. My uncle Glyn (Sheryn) introduced me to the joys of genealogy for which I will be ever grateful and it is from his encouragement of my interest in family history that my collection of postcards of Barry started. Glyn's brother-in-law, Graham (Batt) worked on the railway and the delights of travelling by steam train with him over the viaduct at Porthkerry as a child is a memory that never fades. The Docks were brought to life for me by another relative, Reg (Lewis) and, after forty years, I can still vividly recall the pleasure that my grandfather Alf (North) gave me by taking me to the funfair.

This book is a recollection of a time spent with my family and each photograph brings back some memory that is precious to me. I hope that when you see the photographs they will also bring back special memories for you – of when, perhaps, you visited Barry as a child – and that you will recognise places or landmarks as they were when you first encountered them. Selecting the images for this book was not easy and, due to lack of space, I have had to omit many photographs, particularly those with more of a family connection. I have, however, included some older photographs to illustrate how Barry has changed since the turn of the century.

The book starts its journey to the west of the town at Porthkerry, the park where I played as a child, learned to skim pebbles and built my first barbecue as a teenager. Next, comes the old village and castle and on to Romilly Park with the memory of flying a kite on a windy summer's day and then to the Old Harbour.

Barry Island is, I am sure, the primary reason why the majority of you first visited Barry and I have included several pictures to bring back memories of those visits. Many of my trips to Barry were to Cold Knap and the bathing pool and boating lake and these places are all shown in this book.

Cruises in the Bristol Channel have been popular since before the beginning of the century and one only has to see the expressions on the faces of the passengers in these photographs to see why they were called 'pleasure cruises'. I well remember being taken for a trip across the Channel to Weston-super-Mare by my grandparents who themselves told me of a similar trip they had made shortly after getting married.

The population of Barry expanded rapidly in the years around the turn of the century and it was at this time that we can see the rapid growth of the Docks in order to cope with the export trade from the South Wales coalfield. Again, I have selected photographs from my collection to give the reader a better understanding of just how busy a port Barry was at that time.

Barry can legitimately be proud of its achievements in the field of education and several photographs have been included to illustrate the facilities offered by Barry in the education of its children.

The town of Barry is also well represented in several views. Looking at these pictures one cannot fail to be impressed by the sheer number of shops in the town in the early 1900s. On my visits to Barry as a child, I was impressed by the number of churches in evidence. I have selected photographs of merely a few.

Cadoxton, which has always held a certain mystery for me, is also represented by a number of photographs and I am particularly pleased to be able to include two school photographs taken around 1901.

The final short section is made up of family photographs, mainly loaned to me by Uncle Glyn's son, Wyndham (Sheryn), to whom I would like to express my gratitude.

I am well aware that the arrival of the holiday camp drew large numbers of visitors to the area who would not otherwise have had a link with Barry. I have not included pictures of the camp in this volume; this is not an oversight merely a restriction on space.

Finally, I trust that you will have as much pleasure in reading the book as I have had in compiling it.

Geoffrey A. North
July 1996

Geoffrey North is an accountant living in Churchdown in Gloucestershire. He was brought up in Rumney Village where members of his family still live. His sons and grandchildren also live in the area. His hobbies include local and military history, genealogy and photography. He enjoys travelling but above all he likes to spend time with his family, including a mad English Setter called 'Pepper'.

One

Porthkerry Park

Cwmkiddy was once a parish in its own right but, with the decline of its population in the fourteenth century, it was amalgamated with Porthkerry. The village of Cwmkiddy was incorporated into Porthkerry Park by the Romilly family in the 1840s. In this exercise the remaining buildings, with the exception of the farmhouse, were demolished to allow for the landscaping of the park. The Barry mill was also to be found in the woodland of the park. The estates of Barry and Porthkerry were purchased by Sir Samuel Romilly in 1812.

Porthkerry church, *c.* 1915, which was originally within the Lordship of Penmark. The Rectors of Porthkerry served the parochial chapel at Barry until 1674 and, because of its small population, Barry church was later reunited with Porthkerry in 1839.

Porthkerry Park, seen here around 1930, was landscaped by the Romilly family in the 1840s and has remained little changed since that time.

This picture could have been taken today but, in fact, it appeared on a postcard in 1905.

The long drive through the park gives some impression of its size, c. 1915. The Porthkerry estate, purchased in 1812, consisted of some 1,950 acres.

To the right of this picture, taken around 1915 can be seen the railway signals on the line which travelled over the viaduct from Barry towards Rhoose.

The estate cottage (centre of this photograph, c. 1905) is found in the middle of Porthkerry Park surrounded by woodland.

It is difficult to imagine a more idyllic picture than this view from the 1930s, which shows in closer detail the cottage in the previous picture.

PORTHKERRY PARK BARRY

Porthkerry Park showing a section of the Vale of Glamorgan railway. The railway ran from Coity Junction to Barry, a distance of approximately twenty-one miles.

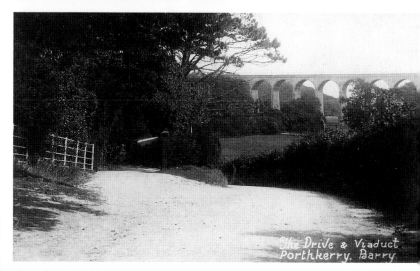

The viaduct at Porthkerry Park (pictured here, *c.* 1915) remains as a monument to the industrial heritage of the area. It consists of sixteen stone arches – thirteen of 50 ft and three of 45 ft. The maximum height is 110 ft.

Construction of the viaduct started in 1894 but, because of problems with subsidence and several collapses, it was not completed until the end of 1897. In 1898 a further collapse caused a temporary closure and it was not reopened until 1900.

Two

The Old Village, Romilly Park and the Old Harbour

The Old Village of Barry was actually smaller than Cadoxton and in 1841 boasted merely twelve households. Forty years later there were still only about twenty houses and a population of less than one hundred. Then, with the development of the Docks, the population grew rapidly and the consequent demand for housing changed the face of Barry forever. Barry does however retain some green areas, one of which, Romilly Park, holds particularly fond memories for me. The Old Harbour, which is a tidal estuary separating the Island from the mainland, was still in use up to the turn of the twentieth century.

Barry Castle. The castle overlooked the Old Harbour and the Channel. This postcard, c. 1900, shows the thirteenth-century gateway.

The Gorsedd Circle above Romilly Park was built in 1920 to celebrate the Royal National Eisteddfod of Wales held that year in Barry.

This photograph, taken around 1905, shows the row of labourers' cottages built by the Romilly Estate, c. 1860.

The labourers' cottages, together with Jordan's Cottage, c. 1902.

Jordan's Cottage, which has long past been demolished, is pictured here around 1900. It was built by the Jones Estate about 1800.

Barry, Old Village Road.

By 1911, the Romilly Estate had built much additional housing in Barry, including these fine houses opposite the original labourers' cottages.

Romilly Road, Barry

Two of the many churches built to serve the community can be seen in this view of Romilly Road, *c.* 1924.

This postcard of Porthkerry Road, dated 1905, shows yet more evidence of the number of churches built to accommodate the needs of the population of Barry early last century.

Some idea of the extent of Romilly Park can be seen from this photograph, taken around 1916.

A magnificent view looking from Romilly Park towards the Old Harbour and Bristol Channel. Some landscaping of the park, as well as housing development, has taken place since this scene was recorded in 1909.

The houses overlooking Romilly Park (top right of picture), *c.* 1915. They also enjoy magnificent views of the Bristol Channel.

GLADSTONE ROAD BARRY

The new houses along Gladstone Road, 1914.

The elegant bandstand and walk at Romilly Park, *c.* 1910.

The Parade Café is shown here, to the right of picture, *c.* 1960. It enjoyed an enviable site with views of the Old Harbour.

The Parade gardens overlooking the Old Harbour, *c.* 1950 – a quiet retreat.

At the time that this photograph was taken, about 1901, the Old Harbour was still in use. The coal wagons in the railway sidings to the left of the picture provide some idea of the extent of the coal trade at this time.

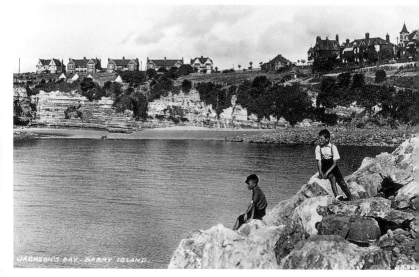

Children enjoying the rocks at Jackson's Bay, c. 1934.

This photograph of the huts provides a glimpse of the conditions and extent of Buttrill's Camp about 1910.

Three

Barry Island

The seaside resort of Barry Island has been enjoyed by thousands since the 1860s. Much development took place in the 1890s and I am sure that the following photographs will hold happy memories for many readers. I well remember building sand castles, riding on the donkeys, eating candyfloss and, of course, enjoying the fun fair.

This view of the centre of Barry Island was taken around 1950. To the centre left of the picture can be seen two nurses at the entrance to the first-aid hut. The fairground and scenic railway are to the left and advertisements for the Ritz Café, Guest House and Ice Cream Parlour can be seen. To the right are the promenade, gardens and beach.

The gardens are seen here in 1932. Several features, including floral clocks, have brought pleasure to trippers for many years.

Dorothy Arcade, c. 1913. Many readers will have visited Dorothy Café, the penny arcade and shops in this block.

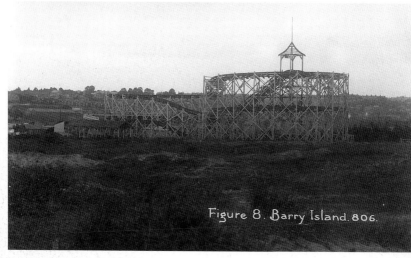

The Figure-8 Railway, from a distance, shortly after its construction in 1912.

The Figure-8 Railway was a popular attraction until its replacement in 1939 by the Scenic Railway.

rry Island, Figure 8 and Show Ground.

This photograph, taken around 1925, captures all the fun of the fair. The Figure-8 Railway is prominent in this scene but also of note are Madame Lara's hut and the Jungle Monkeys. By 1930, Pat Collins had taken over the main showground from White Bros.

This aerial photograph of the funfair shows the extent of the attractions on offer in the 1950s.

Children playing at Friar's Point, c. 1895. The wooden pier ran into Whitmore Bay and was erected by Francis Crawshay. It was demolished in 1902.

The bathing pool at high tide, c. 1916.

BATHING POOL & FRIARS POINT, BARRY ISLAND. 219257

The bathing pool was a very popular attraction for visitors as can be seen in this later view from around 1926.

The ladies' bathing houses, c. 1913. They were built in 1905 together with similar facilities for the men.

Barry Island, 1920s, with most of the large numbers of visitors well wrapped up against the cold.

Bathing Pool, Barry Island.   M. 248.

This view of the bathing pool was taken from Friar's Point, around 1936. Visible, in the background, is the promenade shelter.

General View Beach. Barry Island.   M. 248.

Many visitors to the beach took the opportunity to take short trips around the bay in the small boats seen here around 1924.

The promenade, shelter and beach, c. 1936. To the far right of the picture can be seen the mobile bathing huts which were a popular feature of the beach for many years.

Record Crowd on Barry Island

The crowd pictured here shows the popularity of Barry Island. On August Bank Holiday Monday, 1896, it is recorded that between 30,000 and 40,000 people visited!

This picture should be contrasted with a modern day photograph of a crowded Barry Island beach. The main attraction in the 1950s was the bracing air. It was some years later before the removal of outer garments while sunbathing became generally acceptable and practised.

The bathing pool, c. 1910, very few bathers in view. The notion of 'beachwear' is a fairly recent development as the appearance of these Edwardian visitors to Barry Island illustrates.

Visitors here enjoy a bathe in the sea, c. 1913.

Paddling appears to have been extremely popular here in 1912.

The practice of auctioning spaces on the beach for stalls and swings ended in 1923. This photograph taken around 1911 shows just how popular these stalls were.

The attraction of a sandy beach is not lost on the crowd seen here in the 1920s.

Children enjoying a visit to the beach, c. 1909.

Work started on the sea wall and promenade in 1922. Prior to this date a low wall and railings ran along the beach.

Donkey riding on the beach was as popular with children in 1905 as it was more than half a century later.

Barry beach, c. 1905. In 1897, Barry Urban District Council ordered those looking after the donkeys to wear blue waistcoats, trousers and caps and the donkeys had to carry registration numbers.

The bridge, gardens and promenade, *c.* 1950.

As a child, I well remember the realisation that once I had walked under the bridge I was on the beach! This view dates from the 1950s.

The Dingle, Barry Island.

This view of the Dingle, in about 1930, illustrates just how magnificent the construction of the promenade was.

Beach and Sea Wall, Promenade, Barry Island.   M. 248.

Bathing huts on the beach in the 1920s testify to an era long past. In slightly earlier times the bathing huts would have been pushed into the sea to allow the occupants to enter the water without being observed.

The view from Nell's Point provides a fine panoramic view of the sands at Whitmore Beach.

The terraces above the promenade, c. 1930.

A floral clock can be seen in this view of the promenade, *c.* 1930.

The Punch and Judy tent entertains a group of children on the sands, *c.* 1930.

rry Island: Beach looking towards Friars Point.

On the day that this photograph was taken in the 1920s there was hardly room to stand up on the beach! Towards Friars Point can be seen the café where many holidaymakers enjoyed a snack while on the beach. Other visitors are seen enjoying a picnic, simply relaxing or paddling.

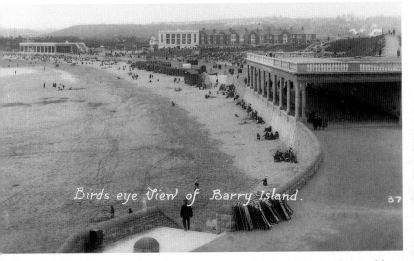

Birds-eye View of Barry Island.

A bird's eye view of the beach clearly showing the substantial shelter which was a feature of the development of the promenade.

THE SANDS BARRY ISLAND Nº 99.

The beach, c. 1913.

62623.JV

This charming photograph of children on the beach was taken around 1917. The pleasure that children gain from a day at the seaside has not changed since that time although the fashions certainly have!

Paddling was as popular a pastime in 1921, the year that this card was sent, as it is today.

Barry Island Promenade.

Many changes have occurred since this photograph was taken in 1915.

Promenade Entrance, Barry Island.

It is thought that this picture of the promenade entrance dates from 1904. The building to the left of the children is the toll entrance to the the half-penny promenade. This overlooked the swings and stalls which were allowed on the beach until 1923 when the new promenade was constructed.

Four

Cold Knap

Cold Knap was acquired by Barry Council from the Romilly Estate in the 1920s. The beautiful pebble beach remains unaltered but there was much development, not least the building of a lido and boating lake, which was to become a popular meeting place for my family, and many others, in the late 1950s and 1960s.

The development of this area proved quite controversial and there was strong feeling as to whether the resort should, in fact, be developed at all. However, the slump in the local economy due to the decline of Barry Dock as a port had created high unemployment in the area and the eventual, successful development of the site created many desperately needed new jobs.

VIEW OF COLD KNAPP & PEBBLE BEACH SHOWING VIADUCT, BARRY. S902A.

Cold Knap and the pebble beach in 1912.

OLD HARBOUR, COLD KNAP, BARRY.

The Watchtower was built around 1865 and was used as a coastguard station until 1906. The picture dates from the late 1940s.

Looking towards the railway viaduct at Porthkerry, this photograph of the pebble beach at Cold Knap was taken around 1927.

THE PEBBLE BEACH, BARRY ISLAND.

219264

The pebble beach, c. 1934. Despite the large numbers of people walking on the beach it remains today an area of tranquillity appreciated by the many visitors.

A child throws pebbles into the sea, c. 1930.

Visitors relaxing on the beach, 1930s. This picture shows the steepness of the beach which can be deceptive to the unwary visitor.

The lake and gardens, c. 1934.

A second view of the gardens at Cold Knap in 1934.

Visitors strolling around the lake in 1932.

This view of the lake looking towards the bungalows was taken in 1926.

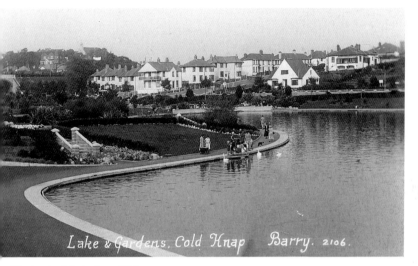

The boating lake in about 1935.

As a child, I enjoyed the independence of the paddle boats on the lake. One of these can be seen to the left of this picture, c. 1930.

Some impressive developments to the tourist amenities, *c.* 1935.

Rowing around the lake, *c.* 1935.

Lake and Shelter, Barry.

M. 248.

The large size of the lake can be clearly seen in this view from around 1935.

BOATING LAKE AND BATHING POOL COLD KNAP, BARRY ISLAND.

W. 1204.

Looking from the lake towards the bathing pool, c. 1954.

The swimming pool where, as a boy, along with many others, I learned to swim.

View of the boating lake looking towards the pool, *c.* 1954.

The boating lake was built in 1926 and was designed in the shape of a Welsh harp.

This view looking towards the lake was taken around 1930.

The Lake from Knap House, Barry.

In addition to the attractions of boating, there was also the delight of the camping holiday experience. This picture, it is believed, shows a group of boy scouts from the Midlands in 1935.

Prom. & Pebble Beach, Barry (Cold Knap.) 77

The final photograph in this section was taken in 1929 and gives some idea of the extent of the pebble beach available to visitors.

Five

Pleasure Cruises on the Bristol Channel

In 1896, the Barry Railway Company gained authorisation to continue their line to the western breakwater. This last section, which was opened in the summer of 1899, enabled passengers to board the pleasure cruises via a floating pontoon. Later a pier station was built.

Barry was ideally suited as a port for paddle steamers because of the 13ft minimum depth in the port. The venture was not without difficulties, however, as the Barry Railway Company was not able to obtain authorisation to run its own steamers until 1904 and even then certain restrictions were imposed. The company was not allowed to carry cargo and could only take passengers to ports within the Barry/Weston and the Swansea/Ilfracombe limits and was excluded from the profitable Bristol route which was serviced by P. & A. Campbell who had been transporting goods, as well as passengers, since 1893.

The Barry Railway Company provided the service between 1905 and 1910 but consistently lost money. In 1910, it sold its fleet of steamers. The Bristol Channel Boats Co. attempted to provide some cruising facilities in 1910 and 1911 but this was also uneconomic. From 1921 until the 1970s, with the exception of the war years, P. & A. Campbell held a virtual monopoly in the Channel. It is interesting to note that prior to 1914 over 55,000 passengers embarked at Barry pier each year.

A pleasure boat returning to Barry pier. This card was posted in 1967 but the photograph is actually much older, dating from about 1930.

A paddle steamer moored at the pier in 1907.

A view of Barry harbour, *c.* 1930.

The PS *Gwalia* is seen here on 8 July 1909. It was sold the following year to the Barrow-in-Furness Railway Company.

Passengers seen here on the PS *Barry*, 29 August 1908. What a splendid parade of dress styles worn for a boat trip!

BARRY.
AUG. 29.

The start of another cruise aboard the PS *Gwalia*, 28 July 1904.

The PS *Cambria* of the P&A Campbell fleet arriving at Barry in August 1909.

The end of an exciting day as passengers disembark from the PS *Gwalia* in August 1909.

The height of fashion, 1 July 1914. It is interesting to note that it was not just the ladies who were wearing hats. Indeed, it was common for all men to wear hats up until the 1950s.

On the reverse of this photograph is written 'escape from the coal yard – should I run away to sea?' I wonder if the writer is pictured here and whether he did!

Six

The Docks

The 1880s saw a dramatic change in the fortune of Barry as colliery and ship owners built their own docks and railway to meet the huge demand for Welsh coal. Between 1884 and 1898, two docks were built between Barry Island and the mainland. No. 1 dock covered approximately 73 acres and was built by T.A. Walker between 1884 and 1889. This was followed by the construction of No. 2 dock between 1894 and 1898 by Price & Wills. Coal exports rose from 3 million tons in 1890 to 11 million tons in 1913.

This view of the coal sidings gives some idea of the enormity of the effect that the coal trade had on Barry. Many of the coal wagons pictured here bear the name of Cory Brothers & Co. of Cardiff. Other companies represented are Cambrian, P&D and Gwllfa & Merthyr Dare.

As late as 1916, sailing ships were a common sight as seen here in this picture of No. 1 dock.

This general view of the Docks around 1930 provides some idea of the scale of the dockyard.

The entrance to the graving dock, a dry dock for the cleaning and repair of ships, *c.* 1921.

Cranes at the dockside in 1909. Exports of coal were still increasing and the port was extremely busy.

A ship leaving the Docks, *c.* 1932.

Ships at dock, *c.* 1930. By this time the port was already suffering from a decline in the coal export trade.

This unusual view of the Docks was taken from the Island.

General view of the Docks, c. 1905.

Dry dock facilities at Barry, *c.* 1905.

This photograph taken in 1921 shows that Barry was still a very busy port at this time. Following the First World War there was a short-lived boom, a strike in the US in 1922 and continued disruption to the German coal industry meant there was still a huge international demand for Welsh coal until well into the 1920s. In 1923 the exports of coal from the Welsh (Bristol Channel) ports stood at 35.76 million tons. By 1936, however, this had shrunk dramatically to 16.3 million tons. The reasons for the decline in the South Wales coal trade between the wars are complex but emphasis can be placed on certain factors: the change to oil as the means of power by the world's shipping companies, the worldwide slump in economic activity, and the loss of markets. Following the First World War, both France and Italy, previously significant importers from South Wales, took German coal as part of a reparations package. The difficult nature of the South Wales coalfield, meanwhile, with its 'easiest' seams already plundered, and lack of investment in mechanisation meant that the Welsh 'product', though high in quality, faced increasing competition from the new, more efficient coal industries elsewhere.

No. 2 dock pictured in 1903. The town of Barry grew rapidly around the prosperity generated by the Docks and by this time housed a large population.

Rail sidings at the entrance to Barry Docks, 1911.

A view of the dry dock facilities available at Barry.

At the time that this photograph was taken in 1907 approximately 7 million tons of coal were being exported annually from the port of Barry.

No. 2 dock in 1904 with ships being loaded with Welsh coal.

The *Walkure* of Hamburg, on her way from the Baltic to Natal, turned turtle whilst loading coal at No. 2 dock on 13 August 1908.

Coal wagons being shunted at the dock, c. 1924.

These impressive buildings of Barry will be remembered by sailors from all over the world. This photograph was taken in 1916.

A tug leaving harbour, *c.* 1940.

Coal being loaded onboard ship at No. 2 dock, 1929.

Cranes fill the skyline, 1941.

No. 1 dock. In 1912, it was not uncommon for the Docks to be crammed with ships.

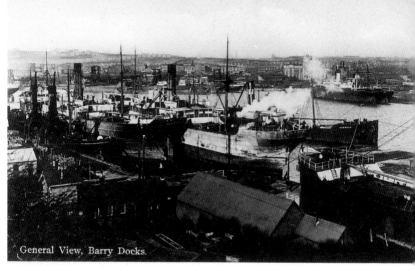

General View, Barry Docks.

An air of activity is very evident in this photograph, taken around 1919.

This postcard was posted in 1941. By 1942 the US Army started using Barry to store goods and equipment and the dock benefited from new handling equipment such as a 50 ton crane.

The General Docks Offices, designed by Arthur E. Bell, were opened in 1898. This view also shows Subway Road.

No. 2 dock with pitwood, perhaps from Canada, being unloaded, *c.* 1910. This wood was then transported by train to various collieries in South Wales.

General View Barry Dock

This view of the Docks taken around 1920 clearly shows some of the facilities offered by the port. Stacks of pit props can be seen to the centre of the picture together with loaded coal wagons. To the right of the coal wagons is one of several signal boxes required by the dock railway. Towards the top of the picture is a ship which has entered the dock by means of the swing bridges.

Opposite above: The Shipping Office, pictured here around 1911.

Opposite below: The SS *Freddy Smith* pictured here at anchor awaiting entry to Barry Dock 10 April 1920.

This view of the entrance to the Docks was taken in 1903. Cranes, which can be seen on the skyline, testify to the scale of the Docks in the early 1900s.

Seven

Education

The education of the people of Barry has always been an important aspect of town life. As early as 1874, in response to the Education Act of 1870, the Cadoxton and Merthyr Dovan School Board was established. By 1910, educational facilities were such that nine schools had been established in Barry capable of accommodating about 8,000 pupils.

Evening classes were started in 1886 and free reading rooms established by 1891. In 1892, a library was opened in Holton Road and moved to improved premises the following year. In 1889, in order to ensure that the education of the population of Barry was of the highest calibre, the School Board took the far-sighted decision to authorise improvements to the conditions of work and pay of teachers.

The schools at Holton Road, c. 1905. When built, this was reputed to be the largest school building in Wales and could accommodate approximately 2,000 pupils.

In 1914, the County Council established the Glamorgan Residential Training College For Women to train elementary school teachers.

The schools at Gladstone Road were built in 1906 to reduce the overcrowding in schools in Barry Dock.

The Intermediate School was opened at The Buttrills in October 1896.

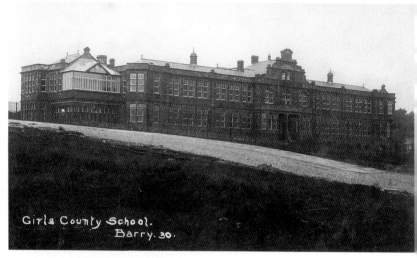

The County School, Barry, 1915.

The educational resources found at Barry were appreciated by both residents and visitors as can be seen from the number of people attending this 'Summer School' in 1907.

Eight

The Town

Barry developed swiftly from a population of a few hundred in the 1880s to nearly 40,000 by 1920. Fifty years later the population was little changed. By the start of the First World War, Barry boasted two hundred streets and the main shopping areas that we know today had been established. The town was well paved and benefited from good lighting, gas and water. Some idea of the prosperity of the town is captured in the following pictures.

The Theatre Royal was built in 1910 and has, in recent years, been utilised as a cinema. In 1921, General Booth the famous Salvation Army leader, addressed an audience there on the nature of the Bolshevik movement in Russia. Over the years, the theatre, because of the facilities it offered, was used for many meetings.

Memorial Hall (2) Barry Dock. 827.

The Barry War Memorial Hall was built by Vickery Bros. in 1932 and was extended in 1966. The foyer currently houses a roll of honour in memory of Barry's war dead, including one of the author's relatives, Malcolm (Sheryn), who served with the RAF.

The War Memorial (2) Barry. 831.

The Cenotaph, next to the Memorial Hall in Gladstone Road, *c.* 1933.

High Street, *c.* 1898. The large number of shops testifies to the prosperity of the town at the turn of the twentieth century.

High Street, *c.* 1905.

The Barry Hotel, 1906.

Windsor Road, with The Barry Hotel, to the right of the picture.

Above: This view of Windsor Road was taken in 1904.

Left: A child standing outside a house in Windsor Road, 1906.

The Masonic Hall (left) is prominent in this picture of Broad Street, around 1909. The building has changed little and is still used regularly for masonic meetings today.

An almost empty Broad Street pictured here in 1905.

Left: Looking towards The Barry Hotel, this view of Broad Street was taken around 1905.

Below: A milkman making his deliveries in Broad Street at the turn of the century. Note the milk churns, no bottles!

BROAD STREET, BARRY.

Looking towards The Barry Hotel, *c.* 1914, this view of Broad Street is a picture of activity. A recently acquired van belonging to the Barry and District Co-operative Society is prominent outside their premises, which were destroyed by fire in 1923.

Holton Road shops in 1916.

Holton Road, c. 1910, viewed from Kings Square looking westwards.

Holton Road looking towards Kings Square, *c.* 1910.

Holton Road, near to Kings Square, *c.* 1923.

J. JANNER
COMPLETE
FURNISHER

ALFRED
JACKSON
SOLICITOR
COMMISSIONER

W.L. HUGHES

Holton Rd, Barr

The activity captured in this photograph of Holton Road around 1899 brings alive the period of prosperity enjoyed in those years. Holton Road has survived as a main shopping area for the residents of Barry and in recent years, as buildings have deteriorated, property developers have taken advantage of the opportunity to redevelop some of this road.

A horse and carriage pictured in Holton Road in 1909.

Looking towards Kings Square in 1922, this view of Holton Road is taken from near the junction with Watson Street.

Buses pictured at Kings Square, *c.* 1924. At this time some sixty buses were licensed by the Barry Urban District Council.

The Proclamation of King George V was read to the crowd of some 20,000 by the Chairman of the Urban District Council, W.R. Lee JP, on 20 May 1910.

The Parade, *c.* 1930.

The Parade. The houses pictured here in 1906 had only recently been built.

Housing at Plymouth Road, c. 1916.

This picture captures the excitement of an outing in 1903. Horse-drawn transport could still be seen in Barry until the 1920s.

The Triangle, Barry Island, showing R.E. Davies' grocers shop.

Fry's chocolate is advertised prominently in these shop windows, around 1908.

Barry Dock Road, *c.* 1913.

The post office at Barry Dock, *c.* 1908.

Wyndham Street, c. 1910. The hospital, which opened in 1908, is seen here to the left of the picture.

The tennis courts in Central Park were once the site of an old quarry, c. 1915.

Nine

Churches

In 1884, Barry was served by just three churches; St Nicholas, St Dyfan & St Teilo and St Cadoc & St Illtyd. At the same time Cadoxton was also served by four non-conformist chapels; Philadelphia Welsh Baptist, Bethel Welsh Wesleyan Chapel, Sion Welsh Calvinistic Chapel and the Wesleyan Chapel.

With the explosive expansion of the population came a similar growth in the number of churches and missions. Between 1889 and 1892 one congregation even worshipped in a room at the Barry Dock Hotel! By 1898, there were about thirty places of worship being attended by the people of Barry.

The Parish Church of St Cadoc & St Illtyd, Cadoxton, c. 1905. A cross later was erected in the churchyard in memory of the 109 men of Cadoxton who were killed in the First World War.

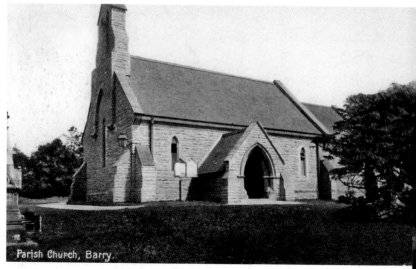

St Nicholas Parish Church, c. 1909.

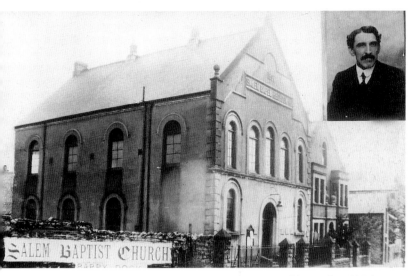

Salem Baptist church, Barry Dock. Barry Temperance Choir practised here and in 1897 they won a first prize at the National Temperance Festival held at Crystal Palace.

Barry church and hall, c. 1902.

St Baruch's church, Barry Island, 1910. The original chapel was reputed to contain the grave of St Baruch (alias Finbarr), the patron saint of Cork.

Merthyr Dyfan church, much of which dates from the thirteenth century (c. 1905).

114

Interior of St Helen's church, Barry Dock, c. 1910. This view demonstrates the simplicity of the design of the church. The font can be seen to the right of the picture.

St Cadoc's church, Cadoxton, *c.* 1900. To the left can be seen The Three Bells' Inn which, together with The Wenvoe Arms and The King William IV, contributed much to the social life of the village. The nave and part of the tower of the church were restored in 1885. A cross was erected in 1922 to commemorate the Cadoxton men who fell in the First World War. It was inaugurated with a service conducted by the Bishop of Llandaff.

Ten

Cadoxton

In 1881 the majority of the Cadoxton population of three hundred were Welsh speaking and mainly involved in farming. The village, which acted as a focal point for the surrounding farms, consisted of a general store and post office – the home of the Taylor family – a blacksmith's, carpenter's and a mill. There were three public houses and, in addition to the parish church, the religious needs of the community were served by four chapels.

Oban Street, Cadoxton, 1903.

The now demolished bandstand in Victoria Park, seen here around 1920, to the top right of the picture, was a very popular venue for concerts.

Main Street, Cadoxton, *c.* 1908. To the right is the shop belonging to J. Davies with the Crown Stores also on the right, further down the street.

The Old Village, Cadoxton, *c*. 1901.

The entrance to The Court, Cadoxton, *c*. 1900.

The Court was built by the Revd John Hughes and was constructed next to the medieval ruins of an earlier mansion. The medieval dovecote is seen here to the left of The Court, Cadoxton, around 1900. It contained 700 nesting holes.

Cadoxton Common was the site of the first Board school in the Barry area. It was built in 1879 for 72 children. By the time this photograph was taken the school had been substantially enlarged to accommodate the vast influx of children to the area.

The author's aunt Meg (Taylor) who was born at the Old Post Office, is seen here, aged eight, at Cadoxton School, *c.* 1901. The picture was taken by the Home & Colonial Photo Company of Cardiff who were pioneers in the field of school photography.

Opposite: The wedding of my maternal grandparents, Ouida Rebecca Sheryn and Frederick Charles Beddoes James, which took place at Holton Road Baptist Church on 7 August 1916. Also pictured are, left to right: Billy Harris, Carrie James, William Henry James, who was the groom's father and who conducted the marriage ceremony, Tom James, William John Sheryn, Dol James and Hilda Jones.

Eleven

Some Family Snaps

Having already explained that my initial interest in Barry was brought about by my family connections, it is appropriate that I include some family photographs in this book. Recently, in my continued quest for information about my extended family, I was fortunate enough to be loaned a number of photographs of the Batt family and, by way of a thank you, and as an encouragement to readers to unearth old photographs, I have included some of these in my selection for this chapter.

Above: This photograph of the author's maternal grandparents was taken in Pyke Street in June 1916. Descendants of the Sheryn family still live in Pyke Street today.

Left: The author's maternal great-grandparents, William John Sheryn and Emily Hinton who lived in Pyke Street from the turn of the last century.

Opposite above: Glyn Sheryn (a son of William John Sheryn) was, I am told, for many years a popular milkman and renowned for his singing. He is pictured here with his horse 'Posy' and milk cart outside the family home at 47 Pyke Street, *c.* 1935.

Opposite below: The wedding of Glyn Sheryn's father-in-law, Albert Batt and Mary (Polly) James which was held on 23 May 1910 in Barry. In the group are David and Sarah James, 'Odin' and Harry Wheeler, Jane Frost, Robert Diamond, Evan James, Albert Batt (groom), Mary James (bride), ? James (mother of the bride), Rosie Frost, Ivor Wheeler and Maria Diamond.

The Barry Carnival, c. 1930. The Model T Ford, driven by Albert Batt, was owned by Messrs Tibbetts, the grocers. Also in the picture are Albert's son, Graham, and Bill Powell of Cadoxton.

Albert Batt, who drove for Rooney's Farm, Cadoxton, is seen here with his horse and cart above the old village of Cadoxton, around 1908.

lbert Batt, who is pictured in this photograph from 1908, played regularly for the 'Barry utchers RFC'.

milly football team who played in the Cardiff & District League, are pictured here during the '08–09 season.

Tibbett's Dray Horse, *c.* 1915. So successful was Albert Batt at showing horses that he won the 'Best Dray' cup outright. The cup is now displayed in the National Museum of Wales.

In the centre of this photograph, taken sometime before 1920, is William John Sheryn, the author's great-grandfather. He is pictured with his sons: Glyn, Bill, Cyril, Josh, Jack, Idris and Tom